Organic eMotions

Poetry for hUmaNITY

Lali A. Love

Ravens & Roses Publishing LLC

Disclaimer

The messages, perspectives, and poetry reflections expressed in this publication are those of the author only. Take only what resonates.

Copyright @2021 Lali A. Love

All rights reserved. No portion of this book may be reproduced in any form without written permission from the publisher or author, except in the case of brief quotations embodied in articles and reviews or as permitted by U.S. copyright law.
The author or publisher shall have neither liability nor responsibility to any person or entity with respect to any loss, damage, or injury caused or alleged to be caused directly or indirectly by the information contained in this book.
Book Cover Design - Julie L. Kusma Visit julie-kusma.com
Ravens & Roses Publishing Visit ravensandrosespublishing.com
Print ISBN: 978-1-7372998-3-7
eBook ISBN: 978-1-7372998-4-4

Dedication

To all the beautiful Souls that rise every morning with pure hearts and an abundant mindset. Thank you for radiating your organic light, your energy in motion.

Testimonials

"What a life-changing, reading experience. This book is a soul pilgrimage. These poems are an awakening. Lali A. Love outdoes herself yet again in a glorious rendering of enlightenment and empowerment. Love's line, "You can't burn the phoenix," perfectly captures the electricity within this anthology. Her words gave me chills with their raw, edgy strength. This collection is powerful, moving, with self-healing and transformative themes. Playing with rhythm and structure, Love varies poetic form in clever ways to guide you through this spiritual adventure. She encourages the reader to embrace their own agency in resonant prose and ironclad wisdom.
There is an energy here, a call to arms and a cry for peace, to protect each other and ourselves. Love says, "We are living in a fallen dream," and that hauntingly beautiful line will always stick with me. She urges us to find the sun through shadows and storms, and she enables us to find inner anchors. This is an absolutely stunning work of art. You will not leave this book the same." —*Author Halo Scot*

"In a world full of cynicism and tumultuousness, Lali A. Love's Organic eMotions provides a salve of positivity and calm. Lali's passion can be felt throughout this whole collection, and she offers each page up as a personal gift to the reader." —*Managing Editor Kimberlee Gerstmann*

"A transformational shadow work poetic journey. Allow yourself to see the TRUTH and transmute inner darkness back to pure light with these thought-provoking words." —*Author Julie Kusma*

"Organic eMotions by Lali A. Love is a body of work that can be described as touching, inspiring, soulful and insightful. This anthology of poems is a beautiful amalgamation of the four stages of human existence. One travels through the tunnel of darkness and exits, leaving behind the shackles of fear, to be reborn, enlightened with the powerful knowledge of self-healing." — *Editor Rashmi P. Menon*

"A spiritual journey reflecting on purity, the essence of life as well as the turmoil and emotional mire which seeps into our daily lives.
This poetry collection takes the reader on a lyrical trek of healing reflections to stimulate the deeper layers of human emotions and freedom.
The myriad of external influences can sway us from understanding our true selves and being all that we can be, before affirming to us ALL that is possible when we acknowledge the truth of our essence." — **Author Derek R. King**

Contents

Part 1 – State Of Mind   **21**

    Strength   23

    Illusion Of Separation   25

    Atomic Cyclones   27

    Fractals   29

    Energetic Fields   31

    Beloved King   33

    Woman   35

    Generous Heart   37

    Relationships   39

    Our Voice   41

    Giving Permission   43

    The Brain   45

    Wisdom   47

    Existence   49

Relentless Chatter	51
Conditioning	53
Limiting Beliefs	55
Comfort	57
Orange Sacral	59
Boundaries	61
Yellow Solar Plexus	63
Activation	65
Sensual Pleasures	67
Harbor Of Stillness	69
Realms	71
Currency	73
Transforming Reality	75
Phases	77
Imperfect Discord	79
The Shadow	81

Acceptance	83
Part 2 - Emotional Vortex	**85**
Obstructions	87
Restricted Emotions	89
The Abyss	91
Longing	93
Spirit Bugs	95
Fragments	97
Wicked	99
Agents Of Sorcery	101
Young Echo	103
Emotional Vortex	105
Triggers	107
Distortion	109
Phony Glimmer	111
Defiled	113

Power	115
Cognitive Dissonance	117
Melancholy	119
Wounding	121
Curses	123
Aversions	125
Beware	127
Disempowerment	129
Wrath	131
The Night	133
Darkness	135
Forgiveness	137
Catalyst	139
Part 3 – Clarity	**141**
Compassion	143
Alignment	145

Innocence	147
I Am	149
Magnetic Spark	151
Attention	153
Reciprocity	155
Freedom	157
Observant	159
Authenticity	161
Inner-Stand	163
Diversity	165
Lucid Dreams	167
Divine Masculine	169
Wholeness	171
Drifting	173
Gifts	175
Self-Worth	177

Spiral	179
Clairvoyance	181
Trauma Liberation	183
A Symphony	185
The Key	187
Soul's Fate	189
Emotional Currents	191
Tranquility	193
Sacred Heart Flame	195
Unified Field	197
Masterpiece	199
Goddess	201
Higher Self	203
Majestic Creation	205
Beauty	207
Superpowers	209

Essence	211
Choices	213
Nectar Of Life	215
Sovereignty	217
True Self	219
Level Up	221
Sun's Embrace	223
Organic Light	225
Devotion	227
Clarity	229
Harmonic Assignment	231
Part 4 – Purity	**233**
Organic Bliss	235
Magic	237
Fiery Purges	239
Life	241

Star Child   243

Paradise   245

Wanderlust   247

Bravery   249

Salvation   251

Colorful Butterflies   253

Water   255

Awareness   257

My Sunshine   259

Little Bird   261

Mastery   263

Sacred Pledge   265

Mother Gaia   267

Presence   269

The Waltz   271

Purpose   273

Remember	275
Destiny	277
Pure Love	279
Hope	281
Greater Realm	283
Simplicity	285
Complete Being	287
The Universe	289
Renewed	291
Embodied	293
Delight	295
Afterword	**297**
Affirmations	**299**
Acknowledgments	**305**
About Author	**307**
Award-Winning Publications By Lali A. Love	**309**

"When we operate from the space of heart-centered consciousness, every Soul becomes our mirror and our teacher. We are all connected within this web of radiant life force energy called Love."
　　　　　　　　—Lali A. Love

"Poetry is the rhythmical creation of beauty in words."
— Edgar Allen Poe

Part 1 – State of Mind

We are sound light waves,
Dressed as human garment faves;
Our souls like to play.
–Lali A. Love

Strength

We see rhythms and surges of life,
A reminder we hurt, bleed, and cry.
It's vital to feel our intense emotions,
Honoring the lessons as pain passes by.

A greater alignment of love and truth,
Is oneness we cultivate from within.
The vortex where Love meets attachment,
Affirming divisions, contrast of sin.

We must find the strength to stop and breathe,
To grant Love's wish, despite the reason.
Exposing wounds, trying to unsheathe,
Unchaining ourselves from constant treason.

We heal the inflamed ego, disguised as control,
That manifests in disputes, spirits we condone.
Dark and Light, this etheric wisdom let's explore,
Two sides of the same coin, existence it is known.

Illusion of Separation

*We are asked to merely embrace,
our innocence without disgrace.
As aspects of Divine Source unity,
known as truth, a loving community.
We have an illusion of separation,
from this quantum field of Creation.
With programming of limitation,
anchoring discord and domination.
We try to use our personal will,
to manipulate outcomes, no chill.
Never finding the long-lasting relief,
arising from loving ourselves without grief.
When we daringly see past the murky smoke,
we liberate the human cycles and uncloak.
Making room for joy, new growth without fright,
because light is shadow, and shadow is light.
When we believe in restriction and scarcity,
it supports the energy of shame and sparsity.
With a heartfelt release, we let go of the old,
and surrender to higher intelligence, behold!
We unhook inner conflict and oppression,
dissolving layers of victimhood, fixation.
This state of being maintains the injury,
asserting intolerance, judgment, misery.
Where there's suffering, it's an invitation,
to love our fears and anger with compassion.
We honor these lessons to free the mortal,
while feeling empathy with the chest portal.*

Atomic Cyclones

Are human bodies just flesh and bones?
Or pieces of art composed of atomic cyclones?

With nitrogen, hydrogen, calcium, and potassium,
60% of our bodies consist of water and magnesium.

Transporting our hemoglobin with iron in our veins,
With an abundance of oxygen to our brains.

An organic compound that encompasses carbon,
Spirits reminiscent of twinkling stars, we imagine.

We are magnificent souls created by flames,
Masquerading as people with human names.

Fractals

*We are cosmic formations,
Vibrating across dimensions.*

*Fractals of light,
Reflecting with delight.*

*Temples of spirits,
Releasing our limits.*

*Mending broken wings,
While our inner child sings.*

*Co-creating by invitation,
With pure soulful expression.*

Energetic Fields

*Let's weave together energetic fields,
in our bodies that magnetically yields.*

*Vibrations regulating organ function,
with our immune system and emotion.*

*The first field in the spinning-color wheel,
governs sexual organs that need to heal.*

*With estrogen, progesterone, testosterone,
compounds linked to quandaries of a clone.*

*We see red as we experience an inflamed life,
through the base of our spine, sharp as a knife.*

*Managing our survival hormones instinctively,
reproduction, elimination, distinctively.*

*A tremendous amount of artistic energy,
when in balance, creativity flows in synergy.*

*Providing grounding, confidence, serenity,
in our empowered state of physical identity.*

Beloved King

She holds Him in a warm embrace,
As her masculine focuses with a secure face.

She retains space for Him to quantum leap,
Evolving through scattering matrices in the deep.

She softens to His divine feminine wellspring,
Devotes herself completely to her Beloved King.

For He is the servant of eternal life,
Clutching his shield of grace without strife.

Amidst falling empires of catastrophe,
He provides space for the truth for all to see.

She reminds Him of the sweetness of home,
That fuels his vision with melody that's wholesome.

He humbly claims his Divine legacy,
With a gentle touch of humility and integrity.

Woman

A woman knows that her shattered heart,
is the map of illumination and reflection,
radiating a symphony of fragmented
light and divination.

She is a Goddess, a Divine Feminine,
worth more than her weight in gold.
She is a fierce guardian, a nurturer,
with spirit young and soul of old.

She has wisdom from life experiences,
and is astute beyond her years.
She has heart as vast as the ocean,
with resilience to face her fears.

Generous Heart

The fourth spinning color wheel,
is powerful energy when we feel.

Located in the center of the chest,
behind the breastbone, it beats the best.

Green governs our generous heart,
lungs, and growth glands from the start.

The oxytocin created to stimulate,
healthy immunity without a debate.

It's associated with various emotions,
love inspired when in energetic motion.

Embodying intelligence and trust,
gratitude and compassion are a must.

The place that houses our Divinity,
the color of earth, it's our spirituality.

When in balance, we are caring,
feeling whole, fulfilled, and daring.

An open heart allows for purity,
of organic light, flooding with sincerity.

Those who awaken to the innocence of truth,
exemplify wholeness by the fountain of youth.

Relationships

*What are relationships,
And how does one attract?
Do they bring people,
That mirror our pact.*

*Connections are comprised,
Of energetic loops.
Desires built on common,
Tendencies, beliefs of groups.*

*They can be a container,
For pure love and healing.
Or for unloading wounds,
Unresolved, not dealing.*

*We welcome relations,
To feed familiar unrest.
Releasing cortisol and,
Oxytocin when stressed.*

*Are they co-dependent,
Needy or trauma bonded?
We keep inviting the same old,
Vibrations of wounding unwanted.*

*So, let's mend the motherly,
And fatherly hurts that drain.
The sorrow may induce healing,
And therapy may provoke pain.*

Our Voice

The fifth spinning color wheel,
is a vortex of blue that will appeal?

Located in the center of our throat,
articulates our truth with authentic note.

It governs the neck, calcium, thyroid,
salivary glands and parathyroid.

Responsible for our metabolism,
expressing reality through this prism.

When in balance, we freely communicate,
using our voice, acting from a pure state.

Giving Permission

*It's okay to feel
The uncomfortable,
Wanting to escape,
The blind spots within,
Requiring our attention.*

*It may be unnerving
Inverting our gaze,
To loneliness, sadness,
Giving permission,
To feel and shed tears.*

*We cannot abandon,
Or neglect these aspects,
Genuine love of self,
Produces new timelines,
Liberating our shadows.*

*Let's do it for our ancestry,
Division and inequality,
For all residing in fear,
Lost in the intensity,
Of the matrix density.*

*But it's alright to weep,
In elation of the truth,
Illuminating the inversion,
Where presence is the key,
For our emancipation.*

*We are never alone,
Sovereign and united,*

With peaceful resolution,
And heartfelt compassion,
Hope and freedom lead.

With respect and integrity,
The tides are turning,
Observe and see,
We rise, we RISE,
For hUmaNITY.

The Brain

What is the brain, this intelligent machine?
Infused with neurons, pulsing within our screen.
A processing unit, the central nervous structure,
With inputs of data and outputs that rapture.

What is the brain, this intelligent machine?
With short-term memory units, it can glean.
A circuitry running information hard-wired,
Programmed, influenced with files acquired.

What is the brain, this intelligent machine?
Thinking, obsessing, worrying, it's obscene.
Memorizing details, a theoretical framework,
Neurotically converting facts, like clockwork.

Wisdom

*Let's imagine what it's like to exist as a tree,
in summer, we're the happiest we could be.*

*We blossom fully vibrating radiantly,
with confidence, yielding fruit abundantly.*

*We feel worthy, valued, whole, and in bliss,
then the season shifts with fall's gentle kiss.*

*Our leaves frail no longer dazzling with foliage,
forming orange, gold, crimson canopy, we age.*

*With every leaf that falls, we lose our belief,
fully emoting self-loathing, remorse, and grief.*

*When the roots are deeply entrenched, please,
remember never to fear the magnificent breeze.*

Existence

Do we question our purpose, our existence, our wealth?
Feeling exposed, feeble, not loving our health.

Unseen, insecure, afraid of circumstance,
we wallow in disgrace, refusing to take a chance.

Projecting victimhood attitudes and ideology,
we ask ourselves the age-old question, why me?

Slowly, we reflect, clear, and integrate the despair,
taking the time to feel the winter chills to repair.

And so, we engage in various healing modalities,
practices and mantras to mend our casualties.

Relentless Chatter

***F**orget **E**verything **A**nd **R**un, says the mind,*
A recording that plays the loop over time.

It's alert and dominates my everyday thoughts,
Built-up habits of worry imprinted and fought.

It has a language, a relentless chatter of a host,
Projecting worst-case scenarios imagined by most.

Whispering voices in my head with fright,
I quiet the static noise with all my might.

It takes everything quite literally, it's the feeling kind,
A million times more powerful than the conscious mind.

Conditioning

Let's untangle the web of old conditioning,
deconstructing the wave patterns,
belief systems decommissioning.

Evolving inflamed egos without trepidation,
operating from the space of love, unity,
and compassion.

Surrendering with caring awareness,
with heart-centered gratitude, and
our blessed rareness.

May the glory of Creation integrate our vessel,
watching the unfolding of our true potential
begin to nestle.

With intuitive guidance, our reality transforms,
manifesting decency and innocence of our soul
as it takes form.

Limiting Beliefs

We have adopted a belief system, a construct,
That our minds are our masters in the abstract.

The fabric of our identity sewn with finite perceptions,
Forming dependencies on external hallucinations.

The ego paints with contrite restrictions,
Using a dictated method on embossed canvas.

Repeating the cycles of monotonous concepts,
In a continuous loop of self-defeating patterns.

Once we awaken our artist from this illusion,
We realize our soul is whole without delusion.

Brilliantly gleaming with immaculate precision,
Our exquisite dexterity forms our liberation.

Flooding our thoughts with pure imagination,
Creating a magical tapestry of Divine incarnation.

A relentless reminder that we, the observer,
Are in control of reality, the Maestro, the preserver.

Let's paint our existence with vivid poetic symmetry,
We are the curators of life's magnificent electricity.

Comfort

I'm more than the limits society places on me,
The fake borders don't define how I choose to be.

I free myself; I take back my inherent power,
I no longer hide from painful narratives and cower.

But old disturbing hurts, failures, and memory,
Creep in through the unconscious sensory.

I accept my denial, my negative opinion,
The notions of polarity that take dominion.

My feminine energy has been suppressed,
Feelings of victimization, much oppressed.

I commit to releasing past judgmental views,
Ending the cycle of discriminatory news.

It is social divisions that create suffering,
I will use my discernment while buffering.

I refuse to play games that perpetuate drama,
Stemming from the collective's unprocessed trauma.

My awareness is in harmony with the cosmic shelf,
Discovering my true nature, the intact higher-self.

I acknowledge the pain I've been holding; I know,
The comfort of decay will hurt when I let it go.

Orange Sacral

The second spinning wheel of life,
operates smoothly without strife.

With consumption and eliminations,
using digestive enzymes and extractions.

Located below the navel covering the womb,
Denying pleasure when in a blocked tomb.

It's attached to social networks, structures,
relationships, family, and cultures.

This orange field governs our intuition,
self-esteem and worthiness in addition.

When in balance, we feel treasured, safe,
loved in any environment without strafe.

Boundaries

She wasn't aware of the power she held,
The weight of the world, a neurotic burden.
Feeling helpless and lost, unable to steer,
On the fringe of a cliff, the lot uncertain.

By accepting her sensitive declining body,
She gave herself permission to purge the hurt.
Searching for salvation, unraveling the unknown,
Establishing boundaries with her energetic alert.

Her Divine Feminine poured freely with inspiration,
Magnetizing and seeding her sacred internal space.
Protecting her Queendom from reaping energies,
With a simple rebuttal, she builds her safe place.

Yellow Solar Plexus

*The third spinning dynamic color wheel,
found in the pit of our gut will appeal.*

*Regulates stomach, intestine, spleen,
liver, bladder, adrenal gland to clean.*

*The kidneys too, with a hue of yellow band,
directs willpower, self-importance that's grand.*

*Impulse control, aspirations, aggression,
contests, dominance, egoic intention.*

*When in balance, we overcome,
the wounded souls that we've become.*

Activation

The awakening journey begins with an activation,
Initiation, expansion, emotional integration.
A pathway of light starting with dynamic force,
Flowing through quantum fields, for my soul to endorse.

My spirit is embroidered with self-awareness and love,
Honing my warrior radiance from the creator above.
With loving perception, I swell with passionate light,
Emanating brightly through broken fragments of might.

As my calcified ribs grow wings of illumination,
I rise above your shadows and your delusion.
I am magic, innocence, kindness, and bliss,
Spreading messages of truth that you can't miss.

With forgiveness and compassion, I set you free,
I'm infinite energy transmuting with glee.
Radiating at high frequencies to heal this earthly dome,
I will love you eternally as I transform back home.

Sensual Pleasures

*Let's dive deep and question our mental forces,
Without blame or judgment of each experience.
Defining the sensual pleasures of our addiction,
Thwarting and preventing our higher evolution.*

*Desire seeks excitement and instant gratification,
With choices of binging in excessive indulgence.
This is considered as borrowed fake delight,
Temporarily avoiding, masking pain we hide.*

*If we continue to abdicate our integrity, the interest,
And repayment will multiply, a loan from the bank of life.
Energetically upholding automated survival cycles,
In the vacuity of suffering of prolonged strife.*

Harbor of Stillness

Enraged thunder, ferocious lightning,
the storm of life wails, it's frightening.
Conjuring fierce winds and torrent rain,
terrifying as I cower in pain.
Under the covers I swiftly escape,
with my childlike spirit wrapped in a cape.
I hear the shrieks of intense gusts, banging,
with howls, shivering with every clanking.
Rattling the windows, my haunted heart delivers,
tempting me to succumb to the fury, more quivers.
I take quick shallow breaths as panic ensues,
to control the dread, with prayers I defuse.
Focusing on my rhythmic heartbeat,
thumping in my chest, the blood begins to heat.
I silence the screams, the violent vortex,
plugging my eardrums, I succumb with flex.
Comforting the innocent within with hugs,
using wisdom of elders, my system unplugs.
I take deep cleansing breaths and follow,
slowing my pulse rate as I swallow.
All will be well, I maintain my posture,
as I listen to the inner voice, security I foster.
Love will carry me home through the eye,
consoling as the silence beckons, an ally.
Docking into the harbor of my internal stillness,
as the tornado of change passes in the darkness.

Realms

*Our world is transcending from mental perceptions,
of limitations and superficial existence,
exposing fallacies of physical dimensions.*

*Merging the realms of polarity and duality,
our voices arise in the domain of self-expression,
as collective wisdom is awakened with clarity.*

*Emoting feelings of empathy and resolution,
we incorporate gracious blessings with humility,
anchored in a loving rate of a higher proportion.*

*This surrenders the pain and suffering of the masses,
as we combat the energy of divide and conquer,
shifting tremors into purity when it surpasses.*

*The union of mind, body, spirit inspires salvation,
denoting honor and emotional mending of many,
may this steadfast kindness propel emancipation.*

Currency

Good thoughts, good words, good deeds,
Your energetic currency grows like weeds.
Be mindful of electrons circling your quantum field,
For every action has equal, opposite impact to yield.

Good thoughts, good words, good deeds,
Through cause and effect, knowing where it leads.
Clearing karmic debris from your soul's boundary,
Your greatest achievement is to realize self-mastery.

Good thoughts, good words, good deeds,
With intentions and actions, your choice exceeds.
Transmuting your passions within a magical realm,
Guided by a journey of awareness at your helm.

Good thoughts, good words, good deeds,
Securing your being with wholeness that breeds.
Aligning with spirit of harmonious acceptability,
Manifesting treasures with honor, service, humility.

Transforming Reality

My encrypted beliefs,
manifest physically,
transforming reality.

Limiting mindsets,
masculine and feminine,
memories of commotion.

Society deforms values,
with superficial corruption,
male-dominated possession.

These notions of attachments,
based on need, sexual distortion,
force, power, a divisive condition.

Resolved by conscious expansion,
transcending pain and coercion,
balance, a heart's revolution.

Phases

*Let's ponder the phases of life's reality,
the chilly shiver of winter blues and adversity.*

*However, the seasons eventually begin to change,
with the warmth of the sun, dewy rain, we rearrange.*

*In the Spring, we embrace the resurgence with glee,
fruit is regrown with confidence we couldn't foresee.*

*We surrender our command to the intelligence above,
with wisdom, empowerment, we don't question love.*

*Each phase of life brings valuable gifts of experience,
to teach us self-mastery and transformative influence.*

Imperfect Discord

A composite of frequencies is the goal,
Grouped to form a cohesive whole.
An imperfect discord of vibration,

Like an orchestra, diverse with our civilization.
After individual parts come together,
Harmony of love chords are created forever.

When we arrange our extraordinary pitches,
Empathy and kindness become our riches.
Once love and synchronization combine,

Our innocence and truth will entwine.
These qualities form a balanced song,
Assembling a soothing paradise to belong.

The Shadow

An image cast upon the surface,
By bodies of intercepting light,
Projections of you, me, human fright.

The darkness latches to pain perversions,
Fragments of spirits trapped until morrow,
In distortions, judgments, prolonged sorrow.

The shadow understands what we renounce,
Bypassing complex emotions, afraid to feel,
Patiently waiting for us to confront and heal.

This phantom is not a passive karmic ploy,
Punishing as we process our density,
Tis a treasure trove of our sagacity.

Acceptance

There is glory in loving our shadows,
Without shame or avoiding our wallows.

We are swift at pointing the finger game,
Judging others while delegating blame.

Love is the glue that binds us together,
Taking charge of ourselves, not another.

We accept our mortality just as we are,
Embracing the flaws of our luminous star.

There's also beauty in loving our light,
A true alchemist transforms both with might.

Reaping the energy, following our instinct,
Tracing our steps to higher-self that is distinct.

Any trigger experienced is from the past,
Waiting to be accepted, released without blast.

It will continue to surface until it's repaired,
Dividing the unified force field, it is declared.

By honoring our traumas, guilt, and shame,
We disrupt the sparks, the conflicted flame.

Don't be shy to express your true feeling,
It's the quantum surge for human healing.

Part 2 - Emotional Vortex

*Only my pure love,
Frees your moral fault or guilt,
Beaming the darkness.*
–Lali A. Love

Obstructions

There are dark spiritual forces,
That challenge our chaotic mind,
Hindering our ability to be kind.

They are potent, unconscious thoughts,
That have shaped our collective belief,
Mounting human suffering without relief.

These obstructions of darkness,
Act as a black hole in mortal mentality,
Much like a collapsed star in the galaxy.

Its powerful gravitational force,
Pulls in the shadows, trapping the light,
Shaping our state of being with fright.

When we purify our psyche of these obstacles,
We access our third eye to see through the veil,
With truth and renewal of life's simple tale.

Restricted Emotions

Trauma, a portal of restricted emotions,
Trapped in unhealed energetic motions.

Seeking to get our attention,
Waiting for our comprehension.

Attachments to obscured childhood wounding,
Stemming from guilt, neglect, that's conceding.

Imprinted threats of unsafety causes freezing,
Igniting protective response that's displeasing.

These foundations of abandonment,
Abuse and mistrust harbor resentment.

Forming shadows, image cast upon the surface,
Part of the light, holding what we refuse to face.

It keeps our pain and distorted belief,
Our judgments, deception, without relief.

The Abyss

Reverberation, a humming noise,
I hear the sounds of space.
I'm leaning out on the periphery,
Crying for peace into the abyss.
I pray for salvation and morality,
But the reverberation only restates,
The muffled buzzing of the humanoid.

My shadow, my only solace.
Beside me, flowing, dancing,
Whirling around the flames.
Whispering, "Is anybody out there?"
Chasing, but the loneliness claims.

Reverberation, a pulsating tremor,
I feel the vibrations of the galaxy.
I'm leaning out on the periphery,
Weeping for harmony into vacuity.
I pray for redemption and decency,
But the reverberation only replicates,
The muted throbbing of the humanoid.

Longing

Sacred fire, see how it burns,
Dissolving the torment of pain,
As my shattered heart yearns.

Fragments of my soul,
Dispersed through the cosmos,
Split from my spirit's whole.

Lingering for my wounds to heal,
Releasing my programming,
Surrendering so I can feel.

Desiring peace, joy, and serenity,
Longing to be embraced,
By Love's flair of golden identity.

Spirit Bugs

Dysfunctional warlocks that be,
the underworld vermin torture.
Zapping each person with glee,
using resources of horror.

This parasitic vibrational match,
echoes the storm of human discord.
Attracting the spirit bugs that catch,
our beams, bolstering their spiteful cord.

Hijacking algorithms they prey,
on thoughts with ill manipulation.
Misaligning our choices in the fray,
an oppressive cyclone, domination.

Fragments

So many humans, with disjointed souls,
Grappling with misery and anguish,
Undoing the essence of Divinity's goals.

We cry to sleep, clutching our grief and anxiety,
A storm of emotions that brew for eternity,
Perpetuating the traumatic cycles of humanity.

We react to events with anger and fears,
Endlessly hurt, carving our spiritual realms,
Clinging to our survival with innocent tears.

Crumbling with each generation, unfeeling,
Splitting from wholeness, numbing our pain,
Forgetting our power that's accessible for healing.

Piece by piece, we release our attachments,
Resurrecting our light, admitting our darkness,
Like a jigsaw puzzle, recalling our fragments.

Wicked

Stripping away the blinders,
I see reality, with stark reminders.
The flock accepted and squandered,
Addicted to suffering, they pondered,
Commending their deceptive shackles,
Influenced by the elite's wicked cackles.

Many will hate and are persuaded,
So consciously stripped and degraded.
Infiltrated, polluted, and corrupted,
Completely groomed and conditioned,
By wicked greed that is perpetrated,
Asking for permission to be assimilated.

We have been ordained by dissonance,
To speak and fight for innocence.
Using our prayers to counteract,
The poison they infuse, while they distract.
With wicked harvesting programs, beware,
Earth has become one giant nightmare.

Society continues to be unaware,
Caught in the astral realm, as they share.
The limitations of their old belief structure,
Unknowingly consenting, the cancel culture.
The wicked make me want to scream,
We are living in a fallen dream.

This I must try to inner stand,
We need to balance polarity to withstand.
The darkness is merely the absence of light,
An illusory toxicity that steals our might.
A system propagated by the greedy wicked,
Prompted by our frequency, which is transmitted.

Agents of Sorcery

Agents of malevolent sorcery,
That inflicts havoc on our chastity.

Enslaving our utter clarity,
In a bottle of impurity.

Undoing collective society,
Indulging in toxic propriety.

These spirits enable suffering, not change,
Creating widespread human outrage.

Young Echo

Behold our story, the young echo.
Unmarked graves, a devastating meadow.

Collapsing schemes of humanity's blasphemy.
Warriors surviving to see another calamity.

They are not alone; on us they depend.
We must feel the hurt, for injustice to mend.

Grasping our virtue, sheltering the smolder.
They cannot destroy, our resolve sees the beholder.

We rise like the phoenix, rebirthing with the sages.
The past has no control, decaying relic wages.

We fight for the innocent, with resilience and veracity.
For the truth shall set them free, reconciled with purity.

Emotional Vortex

*Time is precious,
tick, tock, tick, tock.
As life slips away into silence,
emotional vortex of violence.*

*I am but a wilted flower,
memories lost, stifled, repressed.
Love carried away with years,
emotional vortex of tears.*

*Do not pray for me,
anguish of life plagues.
A broken heart fearing tomorrow,
emotional vortex of sorrow.*

*Do not feel sad for me,
I'm on my knees to beg.
Fragments of my soul, I proclaim,
emotional vortex of shame.*

Triggers

What are these triggers residing inside?
Sparking anger, jealousy, hatred, or shame.
Are we taking responsibility for these reactions?
Or pointing the finger in the judgment game?

Is it an invitation to examine our wounds?
With a message concealed, of electric wisdom,
Spurring unresolved trauma of false propaganda,
Dismantling obstructions, we hide in the Kingdom.

The martyrdom energy is quite destructive,
It may combust with every avoidance,
Of facing the demons, our inner shadow,
Always defensive, emoting the turbulence.

There are other roles for us to explore,
Instead of playing victim and scoundrel,
Healing, we take back our intrinsic power,
A sovereign hero with a shrewd counsel.

To be clear, we hold space but don't condone,
Behaviors of tyrants, abusers, and narcissists,
Who refuse liability for their unconscious deeds,
Exhibiting paranoid illusions of reckless arsonists.

If you reject your emotional emancipation,
For preservation, I launch a healthy periphery.
But before you vilify my essence, take heed,
I'm not a pawn to advance your splintered sorcery.

Distortion

There is so much guilt, fearmongering, and shame,
Mortal unhealed wounds, playing the guilt game.

The star seeds have incarnated with timeline gear,
To erupt the distortion, speaking truths without fear.

An upbeat mindset, confused by emotional avoidance,
Bypassing the collective traumas without guidance.

These karmic cycles of debris repeat the perceptions,
Of past suffering, dissociation, a total misconception.

We're here to remember to ignite our passion,
Advocating for Earth and innocence with compassion.

Joining our life force energy, battling conformity,
With freedom, integrity, choosing love, uniformity.

The Lion may trigger the masses to demolish corruption,
Fighting for sovereign children with Divine's disruption.

Phony Glimmer

I am stardust plucked from the Cosmos,
Consciously transforming realms of my bounds.
As I shed my Divinity to heal old wounds,
I emerge with wisdom of a thousand prophets,
So, let it be known with elation and trumpets.

I'm a collection of souls primed by sacred flames,
But you begin to define me with human names.
With calcium, carbon, nitrogen, and iron,
I form my vessel, a conduit for my mission.
Particles, atoms, and cellular debris,
Molding a bundle of joy, filling hearts with glee.

Gifting my wholeness as my conditioning begins,
You imprint ancestral sores and defective casings.
Layer by layer my pureness starts to dimmer,
Wearing masks of pain and a phony glimmer.

The parasites rejoice as they begin to feast,
But I won't be enslaved by your insatiable beast.
I remember my purity as I awaken and heal,
Fusing shattered pieces of my heart, I start to feel.

Defiled

Our body, our choice, do not grill,
We're born to express our free will.

Let's not blindly agree to be defiled,
Our precious vessel is reconciled.

It houses our sovereign spirit,
Our hearts, minds, and voices clear it.

Created by Divine laws of nature,
We stumbled into an obscure stature.

We remember, as we slowly reform,
We don't consent to pollutants or conform.

Our innocence is tarnished with confusion,
By forced inorganic toxic intrusion.

We take back our power for renewal,
Transmuting our bodies for the refuel.

It's a metamorphosis of the human flesh,
All the innards, plasma, and sacred breath.

Power

Autonomy and power,
A binary thrust consumed,
With alchemy and duplexity.

Each manifesting as ancient,
Expressions of the cosmic vastness,
And primal bloodline of humankind.

A dance of separation,
A vision of imbalance,
Fractured transformation.

The battle of material density,
And etheric forces of intensity,
Light and dark, a propensity.

This metaphoric dance within,
If nourished by love's embrace,
Recreates heavenly balance herein.

Manifesting the wholeness,
Of these dualistic forces,
Requires courage and veracity.

Cognitive Dissonance

Endless conflict and deception,
cause mental discord related,
to global mass contradiction.
Moods of discomfort dictated.

This vicious cognitive dissonance,
expose bogus selfish longing,
harmful broadcasts, an obsession.
A tremor of trauma bonding.

The culture of competitive rankings,
excuse destructive habituation,
fearful of losing security, wealth.
Biased news obscuring information.

This is due to generation cycles,
of unhealed communal suffering
emoting a sense of inner conflict.
Spreading the pain, a virus infecting.

We can choose to refuse and ignore,
its clashing and distracting reasons,
halting the reflective potency.
Reclaiming our power from treasons.

Melancholy

What are these feelings,
That provoke despondency.
A distraught emotional state,
Cycles of protest, a melancholy.

The profound sorrow,
Causing negative patterns.
Leaving us unmotivated,
Feeling worthless, scattered.

Triggered by loss or rejection,
Of a special cherished person.
Shredding our hearts into pieces,
With disappointments of outcome.

Let the sadness flow through,
Emoting so it doesn't control you.
A vexing visitor just passing by,
Say thank you for coming goodbye.

Wounding

We are energetic beings flowing in motion,
Emitting our thoughts, behaviors, and emotion.

What we excrete into the Universe,
We invite a vibrational matching verse.

The melodrama exists within quarries,
By identifying with defeatist stories.

Maintaining cycles of traumatic inversion,
Padding the void with outer diversion.

Our realities manifest these internal views,
Reflecting our beliefs with judgmental cues.

What we project is simply an echo in parallel,
Of our inner child wounding that we do not tell.

Curses

Stir the crucible round and round,
Mold the salt sphere on the ground.
Make spells bewitching symbols,
Cast ideas on book thimbles.

Beware of words that limit habits,
An eternal bane grows like rabbits.
Swift and persuasive, tongues of blade,
Think before speaking, be very afraid.

We sabotage when complaining,
Constricting, timid and draining.
Using words like try, a curse is cast,
With a simple event that won't last.

They are encrypted, a charge of doubt,
Running failed programs without clout.
Just like a raven that dives in the dark,
The curses are real and have a loud bark.

Aversions

A further mental force of obstruction,
Are aversions to events limiting our path,
Creating a state of repressed emotion.

This resistance to people, places, and things,
Emits aggression with feelings of bitterness,
Anger, cynicism, the resentment life brings.

We resort to blaming to escape responsibility,
Projecting hostility toward undesired hurdles,
Manifesting sickness within human animosity.

It's a masked thief that steals our life force,
Siphoning our joy, inner peace, and freedom,
Deactivating our loving connection to Source.

Beware

Release the expectations,
Of the illusive polite society,
Comfortable in their delusions,
By perpetuating their anxiety.

Beware of the one hunting for relief,
Masking as obligation, the collector,
Of souls feasting on your energy,
Like a parched parasitical predator.

They project unhealed traumas,
Lashing when not sustained,
Ingesting karmic cycles of wholeness,
A tornado of torment to be maintained.

Disempowerment

When we believe in scarcity,
we hand over our powers,
and our lives begin to spiral,
into a black hole that devours.

We depend on the external,
to supply our self-economy,
without focusing on internal,
simply forsaking our autonomy.

Reliant on everyone else,
for our expected contentment,
refusing to take accountability,
for our feelings of resentment.

Projecting, blaming, co-dependent,
thrusting our vitality into retirement,
we migrate into a perpetual trance,
of chronic mortal disempowerment.

Wrath

I cocooned in silence, I won't deny,
This radiant transformed butterfly.

Now I roar in the ethers,
A fierce warrior of creatures.

I cannot be controlled, I decree,
My waters are pure and run free.

I will erupt the perverted dams,
With sacred current, the wrath that jams.

I am an alchemist, a breaker of spells,
Of sinful black magic that certainly sells.

I have alerted the lionesses within,
Sharpening claws, much to your chagrin.

I will not be silenced with a fake bribe,
Forming an energetic revolt with my tribe.

I do not fear the underworld, I am swift,
You can't burn the phoenix, this fire's a gift.

My waters rage with the fiercest of rank,
The fallen will flee, this is not a prank.

For justice has incarnated on behalf of compassion,
Do not harm innocence further, your intent will ashen.

The Night

The night has been misrepresented,
As a menacing beast that's adapted.

The mind has concocted this potion,
That promotes hyperactive motion.

Fear of the unseen is a story,
Created by smoke spirits that worry.

Feasting to sustain our lower power,
Unnerved by the potent magic hour.

Darkness

Stars can't shine without the darkness,
We've been taught never to harness.
Dark and the Light, creating disarray,
Attacking each other, we disobey.

This mystic spirit triggers stillness,
Recognizing lessons from darkness.
Emerging as the goddess of the night,
Healing and liberating organic light.

It is from a gentle space we must call,
Amplifying the glow, love conquers all.
Only then we level up to shine bright,
Magnetizing the radiant sunlight.

Forgiveness

I may be tranquil,
Thoughtful and demure.
I'm holding space,
While you act impure.

I forgive your malice,
Vilifying my essence.
As you disinfect in my glow,
I pray for your innocence.

Do not test this Phoenix,
Blazes of fire and heat.
My strength transforms,
With resolve, resisting defeat.

You may stomp into the dirt,
With your twisted hostility.
Deeds and misconstrued acts,
Will not define my mobility.

But I will love you eternally,
Regardless of your lies.
The flame of forgiveness purifies,
All your deceptions as I rise.

Catalyst

Every time humans are initiated,
It's an opportunity for growth.
A gift from the Universe,
Packaged as a modest oath.

The external world acts as a catalyst,
Sparking the shadows held within,
Victimhood, guilt, unprocessed trauma,
Yearning to be healed, released, and seen.

We shift our expansion and become conscious,
Taking self-responsibility, without negative reaction,
By rebooting our systems to vanquish the programs,
That have conditioned us with society's extraction.

Higher frequencies enter our energetic fields,
Combating lower vibrations that propagate fears,
Liberating the past by renouncing control,
Supplying us sovereignty and jubilant years.

We welcome the growth of humanity's evolution,
Opening our hearts, with abundance we receive,
Blessed upgrades of plasma code activations,
Amazing things are coming, this I do believe.

Part 3 – Clarity

*Lucid perception,
Provides me transparency,
Free from confusion.
–Lali A. Love*

Compassion

The world is emerging from forgoing adaptation,
into global awareness of loving inspiration,
where all is honored in unique representation.

We welcome the change of heart-centered reality,
with transparency, reverence, and respect,
finding the base of humanity's capability.

As we remember our innate reward of integrity,
with tenderness, we supply a place to be focused,
hearts brimming with empathy, growth of totality.

An authentic journey is measured by true love,
nourishing our Mother Earth with our brilliance,
graced by the I AM Source of Divinity above.

This generous bounty is abundance in action,
thank you for using free will and pure devotion,
through random acts of kindness and compassion.

Alignment

When humanity veers out of alignment,
A cosmic reboot ignites an assignment.

To restore the natural harmony we need,
The Universe conducts a life review with speed.

Accepting our phantoms shoved in disgraced corners,
We can't evade our shattered presence like scorners.

A distorted projection of conflict and partition,
We must renew with organic truth for our liberation.

With sheer love, forgiveness, integrity, empathy,
It's how we transform to expand our reality.

Innocence

*If we come together and stand in solidarity,
We rise to overcome divide and conformity.*

*We'll conquer daily battles with voices that endure,
We may cry a million tears, but our eyes remain pure.*

*We have been abandoned, betrayed, and broken,
The catalyst integrates our warrior scars as a token.*

*A calamity is an experience where we were wronged,
But the distillation isn't our identity to be prolonged.*

*The light has divulged, unearthing our shadows,
Revealing the darkness that feasts on our wallows.*

*Behold our inner radiance that consumes the night,
Reflecting our freedom, innocence with truthful might.*

I AM

Child I AM,
Whole and pure.
Scars I bear,
Hardened and demure.

Sister I am,
Brave and strong.
Mother I am,
Giving life with a song.

Unconditional love I AM,
Flowing, expanding, evolving.
Embossing my essence,
Vibrant energy in motion.

Grace I AM,
Radiating with organic light.
Divine I AM,
Expressing my delight.

Magnetic Spark

Our soul has a magnetic electrical spark,
Emitting a resonance, a celestial benchmark.

It determines the dimensional annulus,
Nesting within the cosmic ethernet abacus.

This gravitational pull also carries density,
Of resentment, misery with sublime immensity.

If we choose to avoid the feelings of betrayal,
We link with phantom orbits, replaying our denial.

Emotionally reacting to these lower frequencies,
Vibrating slower, spiraling back into disjoined stories.

Only by distilling we transform our expressive charge,
Collapsing shadow timelines, mastering our angelic barge.

This process of transmutation is the alchemy within all,
Liberating humanity from torment, we will not fall.

Attention

What is reality, and is it an expression?
An illustration, projection, and introspection.

Is it the collective observation that we imbue?
Every moment energized by a magnetic glue.

An interpretation of collective thoughts,
This dimensional construct held by vibrational watts.

Our consensus of awareness oversees the attention,
Asking the Universe to create a mirror reflection.

The act of directing our focus is like casting a vote,
Each choosing the path of how our world will float.

Reciprocity

I see you, Beloved.
I honor your light, your grace.
I acknowledge your innocence,
Which I would like to embrace.

You are not your past,
Or the pain you narrate.
You are not broken, irrelevant,
Damaged or separate.

You are not undeserving of kindness,
Respect and compassion.
You are a survivor, my precious,
Buffing your warrior scars with passion.

Love emanates brightly from your core,
Strong, worthy, powerful, and free.
A brilliant star, multi-dimensional in being,
Painting your canvas with purpose and glee.

You are loved beyond measure,
Just for emitting your luminosity.
Thank you for your presence, treasure,
And impact on humanity's reciprocity.

Freedom

What is God, you ask?
The Prime Creator,
The Source of Divinity with a task.

An expression that's omnipresent,
In all that is pure and whole,
Embodied by the innocent.

God is Love.
Love is freedom.
Freedom is having a choice.
Love wants us to use our unique voice.

Everything else dwells in negative polarity,
From a higher mystic perspective,
The light and dark complement duality.

Both serving a purpose, an insurgent,
That we simply cannot comprehend,
Without using our intuitive discernment.

The dark operates as a catalyst,
To activate our internal knowing,
Bridging us to our higher analyst.

We represent the clarity of organic light,
Standing up for transparency in solidarity,
In autonomy, hUmaNITY reveals its might.

God is Love.
Love is freedom.
Freedom is having a choice.
Love wants us to use our unique voice.

Observant

*The sixth rotating color wheel,
is purple light of cosmic reel.*

*Known as the third eye of clarity,
it directs higher morality.*

*Shifting our perceptions as we awaken,
through the density, illusion, not mistaken.*

*When this center is open, we can see,
over the physical veil where we're free.*

*Connecting with higher-self, we ride the wave,
beyond the five senses, evolving and brave.*

*When in fluency, we become aware,
lucid, observant, and conscious with flair.*

Authenticity

If we commit to authenticity,
We navigate situations clearly,
To attract real connections rapidly.

We establish a healthy boundary,
To offset disingenuous quandary,
That infiltrates collective reality.

The shadows of inorganic society,
Continue the spiteful events of anxiety,
But they won't strip us of our capability.

We embrace every moment with humility,
Our destination is absolute love, harmony,
With unwavering resolve to genuine purity.

When we traverse our soul's heartfelt intention,
With veracity of innocent intervention,
It transforms each moment of human frustration.

We possess the lion's strength and flexibility,
Relinquishing external delusions, we journey,
On the rollercoaster of life's beautiful tapestry.

Inner-Stand

Organic light honors free will.
It does not violate,
Blame or guilt.

True love provides us safety.
It does not judge,
Bully or shame.

Our higher-self alchemizes obscurity.
Holding loving space,
For collective renewal.

As we witness the herd mentality,
Of selfish cycles rumbling,
Perpetuating codependency.

Don't confuse duplicity with sufficiency,
Sovereignty, ascension,
Or pure autonomy.

This false sparkly illusion,
Shapeshifts to delude,
Hijacking movements to recruit.

Beware of these fallacies,
That dishonestly mislead,
Forced propaganda to deceive.

Use your sagacity and awareness,
The intuitive guidance system within,
To discern all information and inner-stand.

Diversity

This life is an opportunity,
Where Love meets us in every breath.
With acceptance, truth, and sovereignty,
The courage to live with dignity and honesty.

To know that how we are,
Is exactly the way we're meant to be.
Not because it's good or bad to gauge,
But it's simply setting reality's eclectic stage.

Painting our existence with our uniqueness,
Diversity, a representation of a higher essence.
Every color of the rainbow imbues the papistry,
With beauty and twinkle of the Creator's tapestry.

Each moment a magical building tower block,
Honoring time's splendor with gifted miracles.
As we integrate our emotions without resistance,
Experiencing the horizon of Love's persistence.

Lucid Dreams

I close my eyes and all I see,
Are shards of gleaming starlight,
Reflecting the universe of you and me.
I soar above the enchanting realms,
Embracing life's kaleidoscope with glee.
I close my eyes and all I see,
A beauty gifted with vivid tranquility.
There's peaceful freedom emitting our unity,
Reflecting the universe of you and me.
I use my awareness to unlock my clarity,
The truth of remembrance encoded within.
I close my eyes and all I see,
Visions of galaxies where time stands still.
Sparks of electricity surge my mind,
Reflecting the universe of you and me.
I feel no sorrow, fear, or animosity,
Just emotions of love, joy, and serenity.
I close my eyes and all I see,
Reflecting the universe of you and me.

Divine Masculine

*The Divine Masculine
is strong and brave.
Living with honesty
and integrity.*

*He feels deeply
and loves selflessly.
He's fierce, vulnerable,
teeming with tranquility.*

*The Divine Masculine is humble yet powerful.
He's wise, whole, insightful
With credibility.*

*Living his life in truth,
embracing his creativity.
Looking for a partner
that fits his ability.*

*Knowing his counterpart
is a gift to humanity.
Flowing in harmony,
grace and stability.*

Wholeness

In solitude, I sit in the dark with eyes closed,
drifting in calmness triggered by divisions exposed.
The shards of light radiate, expanding my perception,
accessing the mystical wisdom, without exception.
This awakening practice is a journey of the mind,
a process of dissolving the unconscious ego, in kind.
Rousing from the illusion of a dreary material life,
consumed by struggles and longing with strife.
We arrive at a sublime level of integrity by clearing,
transmuting our shadows to higher reality we're steering.
Shattering all delusions that we are all separate,
from the oneness of purity and love that we co-create.
This recognition is knowledge of unity's infinite nature,
a gateway to devotion, peace, and joy as we mature.
A path toward growth and self-transformation,
of inherent fullness, mastery, and realization.
It requires courage to break free from conditioning,
to open one's mind to expansion without repositioning.
An understanding of immortal, multidimensional nature,
beyond our body, matter, and dictated human legislature.
Weightless, I float in mediation as part of the One,
the truth is an allegory glimpsed by the glowing Sun.
A totality of remembrance without fragmentation,
consciousness of true essence, without disintegration.
Unified as an eternal blueprint of wholeness,
we're enough with our rareness, abundant by
our boldness.
Our inner child is acknowledged, safe
without impositions,
a purity of fullness that Love brings devoid of limitations.

Drifting

Time stands still,
I am gliding.

Melding every dawn,
with the twilight.

Floating through ambience,
visions conjured within.

Hands touching, pondering,
crossing paths, illuminating.

Motivation.
Innovation.
Being.

Sparks, a celestial flame,
drifting sands, just the same.

Gifts

Rise Divine Feminine with inner knowing,
listen closely to your majestic gifts,
your intuitive guidance that is flowing.

Wake up feeling brave with motivation,
embracing your nurturing voice,
that whispers worthy inspiration.

Consciousness is Divine's expression,
drawing your attention to affection,
accord, tranquility, and creation.

Value the blessings and appreciate,
the unbounded generosity,
of your spirit, do not fear it.

Your highest calling is to follow,
your internal Goddess power,
fostering its energy if you allow.

You must learn to turn inward,
so, you can observe and feel it all,
its loving truth and emotional wisdom.

Self-Worth

What is self-worth, and how do we cultivate?
Is it seeking external approval that's legitimate?
Chasing a mirage, money, status, popularity?
Or is this a self-esteem illusion due to conformity?
To have recognition and value are not dependent,
On people pleasing factors, which is apparent.

Tapping into the whole elements of self-love,
We flow with curiosity and sincerity of a pure dove.
It is our right to reclaim our worthiness, our power,
For a life of purpose, joy, a richness that will shower.
We need to accept our realness wholeheartedly,
With integrity, mercy, tackling disputes with artistry.

We hold imprints in our limbic brain, self-chatter,
Thoughts and beliefs that tell us we don't matter.
We're not good enough, smart enough, disclosing,
Our impurities of the inner critic that's self-loathing.
These voices tell lies to keep us in bondage,
Fears that prey on our worth from a young age.

We worry about other people's perceptions,
Needing constant feedback for validations.
We were not born to suffer and be enslaved,
Our path is to free our shadow that's depraved.
Not contingent on material achievements to sprout,
Our validity of Love is enough to crush self-doubt.

If we're triggered or envious of other beings, feel,
And dig beneath that activated emotion to heal.
The insecurity is stemming from wounds within,
It's an outer mirror of internal state, under our skin.
Grasping these opportunities for deeper reflection,

We provide a compassionate space for expansion.

By simply changing our inner dialogue, we recognize,
The merit of genuine heart isn't defined by other eyes.
Our state of authenticity is achieved with honesty,
By courageously and boldly unmasking our sanity.
Building confidence, embracing patience and grace,
Radiating our rareness is the ultimate measure we face.

Spiral

The ego needs to remain in the loop,
Repeating comforting cycles of pain.
It's secure in this mechanical hoop,
Regulating from the subconscious brain.

Our intuition guides the highest growth,
Through a distinctly transcending spiral.
Mastering beliefs of humankind's oath,
As it propels cosmic Love that's viral.

Our inner peace is extremely valuable,
Don't allow anyone to compromise.
In this emotional state we're able,
To stand in our personal truth and rise.

Clairvoyance

*Let's consider how we identify with past stories,
packed with deceptive fears, manipulated dreams,
an obscure personification programmed to believe.
Once we pierce through the veil of intensity,
we can alchemize confusion and uncertainty,
using the purifying mesh of discernment.
Our intuition, autonomy, and wisdom are gifts,
aligned and guided by the highest frequencies,
accessing deep levels of awareness unseen.
Evolution and change are a beautiful thing,
with gratitude and self-reflection, we can see,
that everyone's flowing guided by their journey.
We are the living, breathing embodiment,
an attribute of the Creator's innocence,
gleaming with feelings, sympathy, and insight.
Enlightenment ensues when we let go of worry,
becoming lighthearted, joyful, and at peace,
facing miracles of profound synchronicities.
We connect with qualities of Celestial archetypes,
through the energetic blueprint that dwells within,
tuning our vision, revealing our inner knowing.
As we become acquainted with our powerful being,
our mental transparency improves which is freeing,
naturally trusting the higher self's focus and sensing.
Our clairvoyance activates our harmonious presence,
the self-guidance that unites with the organic state,
a remembrance of wholeness, prudence, and clarity.*

Trauma Liberation

Life is for the living, to embrace the struggle,
Without evading our vulnerable rubble.

Pain is an energetic tide that allows us to feel,
Exposing sensitivities unseen that needs to heal.

This expressive capacity affects our changing flow,
Riding the surge of division, diminishing the glow.

We unshackle our spirits from conditioned love,
Unsubscribe from realities that negate stars above.

By releasing the wounds safely through the body,
Healing is achieved with deep-cellular alchemy.

This simple act envelopes our inner child, a work of art,
Not judging or criticizing aspects of our warrior heart.

By acknowledging the multi-faceted seasons of spirit,
We drink the potion of recovery that will clear it.

Our higher-self drives this path to trauma liberation,
Embodying love, we calm the tsunami of emotion.

A Symphony

The Divine Masculine holds encryption of Source,
An architect of timelines to higher realms to endorse.

His clarity and devotion to the Father keeps him stable,
A humble dedication of Creator's masterpiece to enable.

He guards the portal of truth and intelligence,
Dancing to the tune of Divinity's resonance.

There is a symphony, which is the Feminine,
And there is a pattern, that is the Masculine.

The Feminine is the magnetic dance of creation,
The Masculine is an electric force guiding her elation.

They are united eternally, future blueprint of wholeness,
While the spirit of the mother tangos in his presence.

With cosmic synchronization and celestial echo,
The Feminine nurtures his wounding from the get-go.

For the structure of her Masculine stands tall,
Erecting musical octaves, the crescendo call.

Her nourishment is the healing syrup of life,
Resurrecting innocence within the heart of wife.

It is the remembrance of love in every particle,
Of hUmaNITY's etchings as physical article.

The Key

We cannot escape our current disputes,
Without integrating our lessons, changing our attributes.

It's uncomfortable to feel the darkness within,
Wanting to bypass our emotions, faking as we spin.

But life will keep bringing us the same events,
Attracting situations in disguised supplements.

When we stop resisting and face the uncomfortable,
We humble our presence to process what's vulnerable.

With this simple motion of surrender, we unlock the key,
To life's mysterious purpose, transforming our reality.

Soul's Fate

I surrender fully into the light,
Even though I'm afraid of the night.

Exhausted, fatigued, unable to sleep,
It's an opportunity for me to go deep.

Emptying, regulating my inflamed ego,
I offer forgiveness for behaviors from long ago.

I hold space for myself that longs for recognition,
Loving each part of me with gentle admiration.

Although the purity of Divinity is already awoken,
I vow to exude my true essence as a token.

I surrender fully without a debate,
As the glow guides my unbounded soul's fate.

Emotional Currents

When emotional currents come crashing in,
Take deep breaths to reach serenity within.

Just like the ocean they ebb and flow,
Stay centered, aligned, don't let them grow.

Let the surge wash the density through,
Clearing and healing for a refreshed you.

If the sea can calm itself after a dreadful storm,
Remember, this intellect exists in human form.

Tranquility

*As you evolve
you begin to realize,
You're not the character
you used to idealize.*

*Things tolerated
become unbearable,
Shifting you from events
that seemed terrible.*

*Unshackling from the old
you stand in your truth,
Accepting the inner voice
from purity of youth.*

*Guiding you away from negativity
that no longer serves,
Into a state of tranquility
that empowers you to observe.*

*As you begin to build
new foundations without cracks,
You live in alignment
with integrity that unpacks.*

*Within you resides the secret
of life's revealing mystery,
Evolving your awareness
as you liberate from history.*

Sacred Heart Flame

A mended heart is the Celestial portal,
for atom stimulation within the mortal.

Appearing from a desert of thorny debris,
with feelings of courage, embracing our plea.

By igniting the Sacred Heart Flame,
Creation unlocks, bonding to acclaim.

A substance released with activation,
setting the pledge that sparks true cohesion.

His flame of universal consciousness,
merges with her flame of Divine essence.

Uniting in higher Spirit of the Beloved,
with Sacred Union, two hearts soar ungloved.

Unified Field

The seventh spinning color wheel,
is the top of the head, with hues of indigo teal.

It includes the pituitary, master gland,
cascading down, a swirl of a magical wand.

The coherence of this spiral to our root,
supplies the greatest experiences that will suit.

Our highest level of awareness originates,
in balance and flow where Divinity relates.

When we're activated, we feel worthy to receive,
insights, epiphanies, the unified field we believe.

We access the data, memories across a quantum leap,
evolving we raise our proficiency, no longer asleep.

Masterpiece

Every morning I awake,
Acknowledging the Creator,
With heartfelt gratitude, grace.

For my breath, presence,
Fiery erratic sensations,
For all experiences, lessons.

For my ability to feel,
Every emotion within,
With harmony, peace.

For my stars, sun, and moon,
The ocean's healing hues,
The mountain's sturdy peaks.

That blessed me with you,
An inspiring masterpiece,
My mirror, it is all for you.

Goddess

Over the vapors of flashes,
The mystic Goddess expresses.

In a soft whisper that caresses,
Our faces with her soothing breezes.

She beckons with wisdom and empathy,
An eternal cosmic beauty of time's mystery.

She conquers the dark night of the soul,
With truth, resilience, brave, and whole.

Shifting into higher realms of cosmic vitality,
Overcoming the dense vortex with simplicity.

Transmuting her shadows with intensity,
Her organic Light's bursting with sanctity.

Higher Self

In every moment we have the right to choose,
Navigating our existence with sacred presence,
Dissolving all beliefs, embodying true essence.

Our higher-self beckons to fulfil this destiny,
Saving the human by upholding morality,
Attuning energy to our Divine frequency.

We're riding the wave of each moment,
Like a bright fearless cosmic surfer,
Clearing space for new things to enter.

Flowing through ripples of galactic surges,
Stepping into the unknown of the current,
Unchartered territory that's transparent.

Observing the path from this birds-eye view,
We feel and transform every hurtful action,
Mastering truths without alarming reaction.

The stories dissolve as we gratefully immerse,
Into peaceful experiences with higher guidance,
Authentically integrating perceived mischance.

Majestic Creation

Fastened by eternal sands of time,
Earth awakens with harmonic rhyme.
The clouds emit torrents of light,
As the wind blows Divine's foresight.

It whispers magic with blades of grass,
The raindrops glisten through the glass.
I listen with awe to the peaceful sound,
Of the majestic creation that's around.

The colorful rainbow sweeps the sky,
As I observe the enchanting butterfly.
This beauty takes my breath away,
Heart pulsing with joy, the children play.

Beauty

I open my eyes and all I see,
The beauty of you within the beauty in me.

I see every soul as a mirror of Divinity,
Reflecting the miracles of creativity.

The steadfast core of infinite brilliance,
Beaming ecstasy of your heart's radiance.

Mother Earth grounds this essence,
Cultivating our peaceful presence.

Exuding therapy, serenity, and joy,
An expression of magic for us to deploy.

She tells of a world with heavenly blessings,
Goddess of realms, adorned in colorful dressings.

Superpowers

My superpower flows in motion,
Feelings of love and every emotion.

With each sadness, I feel,
Removes the heart blockage, I heal.

Every anger and rage I feel,
Releases the trapped anguish, I heal.

With every stress and anxiety, I feel,
Clears the cycles of trauma, I heal.

With every human sentiment, I feel,
Energetically impacts the masses to heal.

Not pretending, numbing, or blaming,
I don't perpetuate the conditioned gaming.

I hold space for my insecurities,
Without judging, releasing my impurities.

Expressing the chaos with raw emotion,
The energy of pain flows without an explosion.

I hope this verse resonates and empowers,
To feel and heal are your superpowers.

Essence

You're a multi-dimensional being with a radiant glow,
Do not permit your doubt to diminish your flow.

Listen to the quiet voice of your heart,
As you trek through this existence, not apart.

Your authentic essence is whole with purity,
Know that you have great power and security.

We entered this life to live our truth,
Breathing and evolving our entire youth.

There is abundance of wisdom paving our route,
Choose sovereignty of light without any dispute.

Choices

*It takes courage
to have conceded,
the collective shadow
that you have averted.*

*To discern information
with critical views,
your personal truths about
theories of current news.*

*It takes compassion
bravery, radical intention,
granting others to decide
their intrinsic evolution.*

*Holding space with
empathy to transcend,
humanity's discord with
clarity that can mend.*

*It takes trust
to remember that choices,
impact frequency of the
world expressed by voices.*

*In every breathing moment
behaviors, beliefs, actions,
guides the resonance
of the human fractions.*

Nectar of Life

Realms of newborn modesty and innocence,
Releasing limitations of significance.

Flowers that bloom in harmony with Creation,
Embracing the nectar of life without ration.

Nourishing feathery beings with fresh succulence,
They enjoy every drop of sweetness with opulence.

Guzzling the blossom's sparkling juices,
While evergreen lands exude love it produces.

The beauty of nature endorsed by precious wings,
Bustling so tenderly the hummingbird sings.

A childlike spectacle of Divine's symphony,
Exuding with joy on roads of serendipity.

Securing landscapes of harmonious synergy,
Compressed in vast form of Celestial trilogy.

Sovereignty

*I will not salvage you, beloved
You are not incapable.*

*I will not remedy you, beloved
You are not shattered.*

*I will not restore you, beloved
You are not fractured.*

*I see you in your wholeness
Beautiful prism, radiant and free.*

*I will guide you through the darkness
United as multi-dimensional beings.*

*Take my hand and rise, beloved
Remembering your sovereignty.*

True Self

*I am pure, I am sensual,
balanced, nourished, and powerful,
confident, nurturing, beautiful.*

*I am strong and sensitive,
I embrace my feminine energy,
my true self, steady in flawless harmony.*

*I accept myself completely,
I am a perfect wholeness of being,
a symmetry of unified flowing.*

*I love and appreciate myself as I am,
my identity is not firmly fastened,
to biased social character stated.*

*I am learning, truthfully growing,
every label I attach and inherit,
disguises my real infinite spirit.*

*I am wise and I see realness,
as I express myself in union of forces,
with every present memory it endorses.*

*I am filled with greatness and presence,
my awareness is found in stillness of motion,
lifting me higher to untainted emotion.*

Level Up

Anytime we rise, level up,
Older energies try to trump,
Healthy boundaries we set up.

Like itchy mosquitoes, they disrupt,
Inner peace, intending to corrupt,
Disregarding edges that obstruct.

Throw away the guilt of old,
Blocking us from being bold,
Insecure timelines will unfold.

Respect our borders and essence,
Give us room to grow our presence,
While we soar out of turbulence.

We calm the storm of initiation,
Preserving the freedoms of each nation,
Steadying our DNA activation.

When our hearts reflect our healing,
It's revealed in eyes with feeling,
Melting all sorrow that's peeling.

Sun's Embrace

Let your heart soften,
And feel the warmth,
Of the sun's embrace.

Don't allow the pain,
To deluge your cup,
With anger and hate.

Don't identify,
With the bitterness,
That steals your sweetness.

For morn is never,
Guaranteed so let's,
Breathe, and be present.

Organic Light

I am worthy, I am Light,
I love my innocence with my entire might.

I am a reflection of Divine's expression,
Created and stitched with loving perfection.

I set the standards for what I attract,
I don't chase what's meant for me to distract.

I am limitless joy, with pure potentiality,
My resolve is fortified with tranquil ability.

With compassion and kindness, a Light Warrior of Peace,
I am in service, fulfilling my soul's mission with ease.

In humility and grace, soaring as love in action,
I radiate at high frequencies of organic light and attraction.

Devotion

My love transcends fear with poise and humility,
Existing in the infinite field of conscious community.

A supporting principle behind everything in nature,
Encouragement provided by higher-self as we mature.

There is reason for presence, a pure essence of being,
The more we give abundantly, more kindness we'll be seeing.

Exposing our vulnerability, granting thanks while holding space,
Selfless love is the template for emerging devotion and grace.

With gratitude, we acknowledge our completion of self,
Connecting at deepest levels where Divinity unites with itself.

Clarity

*Looking back, I can now see the inverses,
What I once identified as harmful curses.*

*Were my blessings camouflaged, a gift,
I previously perceived as a wicked rift.*

*It was a fractured spirit trying to trigger me,
So, I could decode my heart and finally see.*

*What I couldn't relinquish or forgive,
Is now set free, not acting combative.*

*This higher power returned me to wholeness,
Uniting my spirit through people with boldness.*

*Crushing me to the core it empowered my goal,
With fierce enlightenment, dark night of the soul.*

*I woke up with clarity, a realization,
That I'm a sentient being, choosing incarnation.*

*Discharging me from bondage with my inherent freedom,
Co-creating my existence in my loving Queendom.*

Harmonic Assignment

Bursting with pure cosmic vitality,
We become the magnetic synergy.
Locating gems hidden in perspectives,
Merging each potential of liberty.

Giving our choice away, empties the cup,
Shrinking to appease others' tendency.
The frequency emitted from this state,
Projects a signal, co-dependency.

By default, thrusting into slower certainty,
When we consent to disseminate our power.
Gravitating to lower electric charges,
Attaching to greedy attitudes that scour.

It's important to expand our sovereign reality,
Enabling our vessel to cleanse with maturity.
We elevate to play in abundant autonomy,
With other creators that emulate our purity.

Life mirrors our sensitive transmission,
Enlarging our magnetic resonance.
Liberating our emotions from self-bondage,
With inner alchemy, igniting remembrance.

Transcending every moment that time brings,
Fearless and peaceful, emitting our strength.
We surrender, release our resistance,
To the partial existence at length.

From this state of truth and clarity,
Free from selecting misalignment.
We emerge as energy in motion,
Picking bliss and harmonic assignment.

Part 4 – Purity

Her heart is pure and rightful,
Filled with kindness that's insightful.
She guards with pride,
to heal and guide.
Nature's beauty is delightful.
–Lali A. Love

Organic Bliss

*Life takes us on a journey,
to find love's organic bliss.
It's a hidden treasure gifted,
as Divine's blessed kiss.*

*Every day is a miracle,
with every breath we take.
Including risks, and choices,
that we ultimately make.*

*It's the kindness of a stranger,
your baby's sweet embrace.
Dancing under the stars,
past the vastness of space.*

*Bliss is diverse as our soul's imprint,
an energetic passion that stimulates.
Our inherent creativity with artistic,
inspiration, our originality awaits.*

*Pursue it relentlessly with hearts of gold,
it's a rainbow of love, a gem to cherish.
Overflowing with hope and ecstasy,
a true delight that will never perish.*

Magic

The sounds of birds soothe my soul,
Enabling my spirit to soar with serenity.

Grateful for the gentle melodic company,
As I sit in stillness and complete harmony.

I feel the caress of the sun, laying on the grass,
Observing the enchanting drift of the cooling stream.

I rise and elevate as I witness the truth,
This perplexing beauty of creativity.

Beyond the physical, my heart craves delight,
Yearning for freedom and magic of paradise.

Fiery Purges

Great Mother with plumes of volcanic ash,
A booming resonance that is rash.
Erupting, liquefying, melting old,
Consolidating codes, a lightning bolt.
Emptying her vessel with molten ease,
What is crumbling that seeks release?
Heave all agony and mind delusions,
Fright, confusion, inferno illusions.
Cast every self-doubt, unworthiness, grief,
In the pit of lava, a sacred relief.
The Goddess Mother transforms all fears,
Embers of chaos and hurtful tears.
Using her lush soils, rich with renewal,
Death and rebirth, alchemy to refuel.
Ridding old narratives of suffering,
Creating space for abundant seeding.
Look within for hidden denial and shame,
Not in resistance of the truthful flame.
The child is emancipated with a choice,
No longer victim, liberating the voice.
Loving you endlessly with purification,
Internal energy detoxification.
We're balancing the emotional urges,
By harmonizing our fiery purges.

Life

We are born of Love,
Innocent and whole,
Integrating our body and soul.

Gifted with colorful emotions,
As sentient beings free to choose,
The experiences that will amuse.

With every moment of breath,
We're sanctified with a life,
Bursting with both bliss and strife.

When we align, we become aware,
Of purpose to expand our essence,
The lively match to higher presence.

Star Child

Every star child bestows a gift,
A blessing to reflect our rift.

The miracle that overwhelms with joy,
Setting hearts with purity we employ.

They project a world of innocence,
A devoted nature our souls dispense.

Let us learn from their Divine spirit,
Their truth and wisdom we inherit.

We must protect the sacred liberty,
Of you and me, ordained by the holy.

We're grateful for their cherished existence,
Teaching infinite love to each substance.

Paradise

Hold my hand and skip along with me,
Inside my inner world, come and see.

A paradise where we are free,
To experience life's mystery.

Anything your heart desires,
Blazes with enthusiastic fires.

With joyous prancing, within my creation,
Encounters filled with pure imagination.

Embraced with delight, tranquility, glee,
It's everything your soul wishes to be.

Wanderlust

Energetic beings,
Flowing in motion.

Loving our atoms,
And every emotion.

A radical incarnation,
From the constellation.

The universal expression,
Of Divine intervention.

The holy aspects of purity,
With innocence of unity.

We are poetic stardust,
A golden ripple of wanderlust.

Bravery

*There is presence and absence,
both equal parts of the evolutionary cycle,
helping us clear imprints, so we don't recycle.*

*With bravery and resilience,
we transform and liberate traumas,
to cultivate experiences without dramas.*

*As we learn the secrets of emotional freedom,
we operate from the space of Love's vibration,
not pretending, with an elusive foundation.*

*In each layer of sensation, we question,
the relationship of feelings, thoughts, a reflection,
is it a connection of opposition or affection?*

*Unpacking the complexities of existence,
evolving our mastery and unending capacity,
integrating our hearts and minds is essential.*

*So, let's beam our natural starlight nobly,
illuminating a transcending society,
displaying radiance of Love's unanimity.*

Salvation

Salvation is found through heart-centered purity,
With truth, genuine love washes impurity.

The living word of Source is the Creation of all,
A spirit in you and me, together we won't fall.

There's no need for indoctrination to dream,
Of a peaceful nation, it's there for us to glean.

We don't require a moderator to access trinity,
To merge and connect with nature, central Divinity.

We hold the power within, be still and rethink,
Heaven exists in the sublime water we drink.

Colorful Butterflies

The thunder rumbles,
Electric lightning roars.

Threatening our survival,
As our heartbeat soars.

A calamity of forces,
The battle for the ages.

The darkness and light,
A wisdom of the sages.

After the storm ends,
A stunning vortex transcends.

Embracing the skies,
Dappled as colorful butterflies.

Water

Peaceful water, repair my wounds,
As the shadows cast their spells,
Soaking weary bones, encased by jaded shells.

I feel the relief of your embrace,
The soothing satin engulfs my skin,
As the running river comes crashing in.

With affirmations and intentions,
I purge, release, detoxify my density.
Floating in the ocean of bliss and purity.

My heart is open and flowing with ease,
I'm grateful for the power that enables me to see,
Cleanse and regenerate, alas, my soul is free.

Awareness

In every moment's presence,
We find the eye of awareness.

Within this conscious state,
We create a reliable space.

As thoughts and emotions,
Don't define our spirit.

We don't give them power,
To narrate our existence.

Becoming the master author,
Plotting our eclectic chapters.

Let's honor and face our sensations,
Accepting our shadows and its lessons.

Our higher-self steers each reality,
Returning to our hearts of purity.

We become the magnet of empowerment,
Co-creating a mindful community.

My Sunshine

My life in the sunshine.
Exhilaration

Filled with warmth and delight.
Jubilation

A feeling of triumph and felicity.
Elation

My heart bursts open with gaiety.
Exaltation

A state of intense frenzy and serenity.
Excitement

My life in the sunshine.
Ecstatic

Floating between time's organic rhapsody.
Euphoric

Little Bird

Little bird
Singing in a cage
Flap your wings
And fly away.

Untethered and free
From animosity
With total vulnerability
That's where I want to be.

Little bird
Connected and jolly
Waltzing with the wind
No worries to rescind.

Woven into Gaia's breath
You have liberated my spirit
Igniting my inner Wi-Fi
Soaring me above the sky.

Little bird,
Help me mend
These broken wings
To embrace what tomorrow brings.

My existence quakes
Grasping to love's dream
As my tattered heart feels
The fragments of anarchy.

Little bird
Pure and whole
Your song unshackles my soul
This nature's symphony is my goal.

Mastery

The blazing flames of truths are erupting,
As the world awakens from lies disrupting.

We take back our power, preventing conventionality,
Making choices that don't insult our soul's uniformity.

Upgrading, releasing, and clearing our density,
With majestic galactic light code intensity.

We honor our strength and virtue with gratitude,
Connecting our unified hearts with greater latitude.

Bridging our spheres by respecting Mother Earth,
Entering a new paradise with humanity's rebirth.

We assist our collective journey with gentle peace,
Focusing our profound intentions, actions with ease.

Evolving our natural stability with self-love,
We recall our mastery graced by Creator above.

Sacred Pledge

*Souls recognize each other,
through an energetic exchange,
a magnet for celestial love,
yearning to be rearranged.*

*Their voices whisper,
across cosmic dimensions,
transcending all boundaries,
of time, space conventions.*

*When connected in unity,
they replenish and deliver,
like the sun-heated rock,
purified by the rushing river.*

*They praise their Soulmate,
without words to acknowledge,
a sonata of two heartbeats,
applauding Divine's sacred pledge.*

Mother Gaia

As we look around our beloved Earth,
We simply observe the world's rebirth.

It's destined to shift and evolve,
Mother Gaia ascends to absolve.

Like flawless diamond, the crystals signify,
Feelings so unique that you can't deny.

A chance to co-create a sympathetic globe,
With honor and service to humanity's strobe.

This inspired collective testimony,
Builds the bridge for us to dwell in harmony.

Through heart-centered expansion we rise,
As cohesive conscious group of allies.

Presence

Every breath
Is a new beginning
A reset of activations
A recalibration
A rebirth
Allowing our spirit
To remember the song
Of Presence.

Guided by descendants
To the dimensional
Spaces within
Healing and retrieving
Through Divine codes
They communicate
To remember the song
Of Presence.

Within nature
Each organic plant
A sacred teacher
Wisdom keepers
Of ancient truths
They murmur in silence
To remember the song
Of Presence.

The Waltz

Sometimes we rise together to withstand,
The tropical storm we don't understand.
Embracing it fully and courageously,
As we navigate its treacherous journey.

We find strength and veracity in the barrage,
Facing the ashes of the volcanic sabotage.
Making friends with the dust, earthly shadows,
Taking its hand in a dance with rhythmic prose.

We soar together in highs and lows,
As the storm distills the density, it slows.
Eradicating the malicious harm to expose,
The toxicity depleting our life to impose.

We continue the waltz of emotional release,
The blackness a virtue, the path made of peace.
Aligned to its power we howl in the windstorm,
Twirling, we transform the energy void of form.

We find freedom to propel our magnetic reality,
Valuing the sanitized blustery soiree of mortality.
The pain is our healing, the scream is our song,
Dancing life's choreography is where we belong.

Purpose

I embrace new concepts,
And flamboyant prospects.

I accept what occurs on surface,
That will achieve my higher purpose.

I trust I'm steered to progress,
Supported through the process.

While the old systems crumble,
Their servants combat the tumble.

I am called to simply observe,
As the neutral peaceful witness.

Using my inner light, compass,
In service with my self-guidance.

I navigate through the evolution,
Not from fear, but only with compassion.

My dedication abides the truest spirit,
No longer searching devotion, just being it.

Holding space knowing we are all worthy,
Deserving of bliss, love, lucidity.

These wings transcend profound initiation,
My words are powerful tools of creation.

Remember

In moments of uncertainty,
Recollect your emerald center,
And return to the neutral mentor.

It's easy to be swept,
Into the emotional currents,
The defamation of human events.

Within us we find sanctity,
Our validation and safety,
Home, embracing decency.

This truth provides clarity,
The resonance of liberty,
Co-creating reality.

As the cycle of chaos lingers,
Remember your innate legacy,
You're the stargate of Divinity.

Destiny

Forging our utopian destiny,
We unplug from hectic propensity.
Stepping into the organic sunshine,
The abundant beauty of the Divine.

With affirmative prayers, we process,
Infusing meditation to de-stress.
An open heart ready for surrender,
To the presence of oneness that's tender.

We erupt the paradigms of separation,
Sweeping the entire unconscious nation.
The greed, doubt, worry, and disease,
Will be vanquished by Love's appease.

We recall our mystic energy in motion,
Immersed in joy and creative emotion.
Within this natural synergetic state,
We're free to generate our heavenly fate.

Pure Love

*Pure love is the eternal presence,
that expels all illusion, distortion,
illuminating the sacred essence.*

*What we're reconstructing echoes,
the embodiment of the most holy,
resurrecting heavenly meadows.*

*This truth nourishes the expansion,
of mercy's conscious evolution,
while systems graze on limitation.*

*We are laying out the blueprint,
rebuilding the worldly template,
salvaging our cosmic footprint.*

*As we heal with balanced harmonic,
we attune to the pulsation of Earth,
restoring lands with sweet euphonic.*

*Quenching my lungs with oxygen, I face,
the living flame, eternal life's spirit,
bathing each cell with Love's exquisite grace.*

*The deeper I connect with my clarity,
I am filled with bliss for this pure majesty,
in between breath that stretches infinity.*

Hope

Connect and go deep,
Replenish with hope,
From remorse to joy,
Together we cope.

Fearlessly living in truth,
With dreams of thrill and vision,
Fitting our purpose that soothe,
Luring rapture not division.

When our loving hearts,
Are open to receive,
Genuine bliss mends,
Broken wings, believe.

Greater Realm

Life is a journey to remember,
The unbounded love sought forever.

It's been inside our chamber all along,
Waiting patiently to unite and belong.

We learn the lessons on the way,
Solving storms that clear our path to play.

Self-realization is the source of all bliss,
Manifesting devotion deserved not remiss.

When we believe in the power of the greater realm,
We choose to prioritize our soul, not overwhelm.

Our temples are the sacred ground wanting to seed,
Ending inner suffering, co-creation is decreed.

Simplicity

Changes beckon to help me grow,
Refining hearts absorb the glow.

A gentle, loving, state of clarity,
Clearing polarized negativity.

Reflecting, flowing, and uncovering,
Simplicity of life, not hovering.

These hidden gems of a higher wisdom,
Concealed in my emotional freedom.

Recalibrating my essence anew,
With feelings of unbounded love for you.

Releasing, I let go, the past will not sway,
The phoenix cleanses its residue away.

Sunrise, embrace me with your alluring gleam,
While tranquility takes me along life's stream.

Complete Being

As we connect to our breath, the chest core,
reclaiming soul's honor, forevermore.

We choose our path to gracefully move,
Shifting our unified rhythmic groove.

Each of us embody the spirit of warriors,
Fiercely overcoming all external barriers.

We also represent the caring yogi,
Flowing with kindness and tenderness is key.

This fusion surrenders the human we're freeing,
Combining the dual nature, a complete being.

With bliss in our heart, wherever we roam,
The peace in our soul, will guide all home.

The Universe

*Love emerges in every moment,
In the darkness, it's our proponent,
And in the presence of best victories,
Love holds our hand within the mysteries.*

*When life is expansive and flowing,
Joyful, connected to inner knowing,
Or frustratingly inconvenient,
Love supplies safe space that's lenient.*

*Our heart's the compass of the Universe,
Let's make it the center of our free verse,
Devoting to our own core in response,
To emotional freedoms, we ensconce.*

*As we embody the consciousness,
Of healing our earthly consequence,
We reflect organic light of Divinity,
Back into our heart-centered affinity.*

*Granting innocent child like vulnerability,
The playground of our exquisite ability,
Revealing the powerful radiant force within,
To motivate the master in all that's akin.*

Renewed

I'm soaring with flow of presence,
Unprovoked by the unconscious,
Shadows of people and behaviors,
By banning inorganic permeations,
That disregard my firm limitations.

I'm growing, healing, and evolving,
Emitting the light of understanding,
Shining my emerald heart brightly,
Dissolving the old programming,
Of unconsciousness that's crumbling.

I'm no longer pursuing permission,
To be my genuine loving person,
I refuse to play small in compliance,
Accepting and trusting myself in mission,
Roaming as a renewed upgraded human.

I'm choosing to live as a pure sovereign,
Honoring my harmonious occurrence,
A fresh bouquet of Source, emboldened,
Making astute aligned choices as guided,
By my blissful highest self, it's decided.

Embodied

The rebirth of Love is taking place,
With splendor of vivid earthly space.

Divine's natural law is embodied,
Creating supreme grace that is steadied.

Distilling the old in the flame,
Reviving the new without shame.

We're drops in the eternal ocean,
Cycles activating emotion.

Constructing humanity's renewal,
With the rise of the feminine fuel.

A mirror of gentle aquatic mists,
Purified essence of clarity, gifts.

This journey propels our mortal dome,
Entering waters of cosmic womb, home.

Delight

There once was a world filled with fright
That drank the love brew of delight.
With a playful pun
It recalled some fun
And resumed its dazzling light.

Afterword

We have an opportunity to expand,
the shared human consciousness,
by collapsing limiting beliefs, structures,
cellular debris stored in unconsciousness.
Despite the things we intend to manifest,
the Universe is guiding us through a nest,
of outcomes, emotions, and events,
that is uniquely for the collective best.
This is not occurring due to the insistence,
of our personal ailments for us to compete,
but because we honor the truth of reality,
and uncover perceptions of the deceit.
As we evolve, we recognize the fragmentation,
the viewpoints about this interpretation,
assisting in our awakening to honor the illusive,
and the mysterious process of transmutation.
This revolution acts as the sacred fire,
An erupted lava, humanity's debris of trauma,
every time we are triggered externally,
it's a spark to observe our emotional drama.
With this Universal partnership of co-creation,
we embrace the exquisite timing of grace,
that is doing everything in its infinite power,
despite our judgments and personal disgrace.
We are steered towards our heart-center feelings,
embodying the love, a reflection of Divine being,
to be fully integrated into the human vessel,
that we were always meant to be freeing.
From this space, we come to appreciate,
the true fulfillment we have been seeking,
by choosing alignment with heart, mind, spirit,
releasing dependencies without critiquing.
At this crucial time of alchemical transfiguration,

*the mystical practices are those rooted,
in self-love, purification, and self-liberation.
As the signs of a newly awakened world,
resurfaces in the beauty and magic of life,
thanks for being the catalyst of integrity,
wholeness, by vibrating purely without strife.*

Affirmations

I open my heart to receive the wisdom of my Soul and transcend old narratives by stepping into deeper octaves of organic light. As my heart unlocks the infinite potential within, I am held and nurtured by the intelligent, loving universe. I am a channel of love, radiating golden waves of organic light frequency. I am a sacred vessel through which Divine Source energy illuminates love consciousness. I am powerful, I am free. I co-create my reality.

I have the power to create all the success and prosperity I desire. I can let go of the old, negative beliefs that have shackled my innocence, purity, and stood in the way of my joy. The universe is filled with endless opportunities for my success. I am surrounded by supportive, positive people who believe in me and want me to succeed. As I take on new challenges, I feel calm, confident, and empowered. I tap into the harmonic frequencies of the collective quantum field of love and unity.

I am aligned with my purpose, I feel grateful. Everything that is happening in my life is happening for a reason. I am content with my life and with the choices I am making. I am focused on self-growth every day, anchored in truth and wholeness. I am here for a reason and it's clear to me now. My life is inspiring, uplifting, motivating, and joyous. I navigate energy shifts from the higher self. I surrender and trust in my inner guidance and wisdom.

I am open to new and wonderful changes. Abundance flows freely through me. It's alright to feel sad, confused, or angry. I will honor my emotions and let them flow through me, without any attachments. I hold space for myself with kindness, compassion, and grace. Today, I am going to tackle everything bravely, with empathy and confidence. I release old stories and create space for new timelines to anchor in loving awareness.

My higher heart expands with purity and love. I am grateful for the gift of every breath of life. I love and celebrate my physical vessel. I choose peace. I'm courageous, strong, and powerful. I stand up for myself and all that is innocent. I deserve to have joy in my life. I approve of myself and love myself deeply. I AM worthy and I will succeed in manifesting everything my heart desires. I AM pure potentiality.

I love myself unconditionally. I can feel the radiance emanating from my heart center. I love the way I look, the way I talk, the way I think. I am so grateful to be in this body, this vessel of Divine's expression. I love my life. I am grateful for every experience. I love my relationships and my Soul family. I anchor healing waves of golden crystal codes radiating through my cells as I embrace all my Divine essence and embody my higher self's wisdom. My heart is pure, open, and full of grace and humility.

I am relaxed, I am calm. I feel peace and joy. In every moment I choose love over fear and create vibrations of healing, harmony, and flow within. My mind is a peaceful and beautiful place. I don't allow anyone or anything to diminish my light. I keep my emotions in a neutral state. I observe and acknowledge everything that arises with grace and concord. I magnetize bliss, joy, freedom, and fulfillment. I am a unique expression of the Divine and that's my gift to the world.

I continuously push myself to learn and develop in areas of life that bring me happiness, freedom, and purpose. I wake up every morning ready for a new day of exciting possibilities. I am a vessel of Divine love, empathy, and healing. I take back my power and master my reality. I anchor sacred love energy through my temple, aligning with higher frequencies and my higher wisdom. I activate the crystalline codes within my blueprint. I am valuable and will make powerful contributions to the world to uplift humanity.

Only I know what is best for me. I allow myself the space and time to support my inner healing journey. I listen to my intuition and trust my inner guide. I am strong and confident. I am always headed in the right direction. I put my energy into things that matter to me. I trust myself to make the right decisions. I use critical thinking to sift through the information. I am ascending to my truth every day. I make a difference in the world by simply existing, using my discernment, and loving with an open, compassionate heart. I honor this process through self-healing.

I am a sentient being. I am free to choose my reality. Nobody but me decides how I feel. My life is taking place right here, right now. I opt to rise above negative feelings and thought patterns. I am liberating myself from fear, judgment, suffering, and doubt.

My heart is an infinite well of unconditional love. Inside me, I feel calm and serene. I open the gateway to deeper levels within my sacred vessel. I release all narratives of the past that inhibit the flow of love. I take back my power. Nothing can disturb this peacefulness. No one has the capacity to dim my inner light.

I have the knowledge to make intelligent decisions for myself. I have all that I need to live in peace and harmony. I am and always will be enough. I acknowledge my own self-worth. My confidence is rising. I let go of any negative feelings about myself or my life and accept all aspects of me. I am courageous and brave. I open my higher heart waves and anchor light codes of love. I release the illusion of separation from Divine Source and choose to embody love-consciousness over fear.

Life brings me experiences that I am strong enough to handle. I am open to new and wonderful changes. I feel glorious, dynamic energy. I am active and alive. Abundance flows freely through me. My self-esteem is high because I honor who I am. I take back my power from external forces. I will tackle every obstacle that comes my way bravely and with confidence. I let go of the old paradigms and ground myself within the healing nature of Mother Earth. I believe in my Divine essence and presence.

I am blessed with an incredible, supporting Soul tribe who accept me wholly. Everything that is happening now is for my ultimate good. I am courageous and I stand up for myself and speak my truth. I use my discernment and question everything. My body is healthy, my mind is brilliant, my soul is tranquil and pure. I am learning to trust the intelligent and loving Universe with my precious journey. I convert everything into love through my emotional body.

I AM a being of radiant organic light.

I accept my power. All areas of my life are abundant and fulfilling. Every experience, lesson, and pain are perfect gifts for my Soul's growth and expansion. I AM worth loving. There is love all around me. I am the master of my beliefs that manifest my reality. I don't judge myself or blame anyone as I take responsibility for my self-actualization. I accept and love myself thoroughly as I learn to conquer my emotional reactions. The abundance of love engulfs me as I flow in alignment with the loving and intelligent Universe.

I give gratitude for my life experiences with an open heart and loving intentions.

I release all my fears, judgment, unworthiness, and insecurities from my body. I honor, feel, and clear every emotion that arises. I reclaim my sovereignty and live my divine life filled with joy, bliss, integrity, and peaceful tranquility. Every cell in my body relaxes and functions in perfect harmony with change. I embody my inner Goddess, advocating for innocence, wholeness, and purity. I am a Warrior of peace; I will overcome and transmute any obstacle or shadow that crosses my path. I AM an alchemist, a conscious co-creator, weaving healing, with loving frequencies. I create bliss within each moment. I rise within my divine feminine power, birthing, integrating, flowing with creativity and magic.

Acknowledgments

Thank you, God, and the Universe, for all our blessings and for all the abundance that is yet to come. I am most grateful for the creative flow that guides my writing during these tumultuous times in humanity's evolution and activations of consciousness.

I would like to extend my heartfelt gratitude to Julie, the Queen of Horror and Generosity, for her artistic talents and exceptional kindness, bringing my vision to life with the captivating cover design.

My deepest thanks and sincere appreciation to my friends and phenomenal authors, Derek R. King, Julie L. Kusma, and Halo Scot for their time and patience while beta-reading my manuscript. It's such an honor to receive your feedback and testimonial for my poetry. I am profoundly grateful.

I would also like to acknowledge the Ravens and Roses Publishing team for the amazing collaboration and for providing this book internationally in such a brief timeframe. May it resonate with many as we release our attachments to emotions that create internal suffering.

To my heart and soul, thank you for motivating me to be the wealthiest of hearts. May we purify and rise in hUmaNITY with inner peace, a sense of joyful well-being, freedom of choice, integrity, and wholeness.

About Author

Lali A. Love is a multi-award-winning author, bridging the concepts of metaphysics with visionary storytelling and empowering poetry. Since July 2019, she has published her Amazon best-selling novels *Heart of a Warrior Angel: From Darkness to Light*, *The De-Coding of Jo: Hall of Ignorance*, *The De-Coding of Jo: Blade of Truth*, and *The Joy of I.T. (Infinite Transcendence)*.

Lali writes bestselling dark fantasy, science fiction, metaphysical thrillers, and inspirational poetry. She has received the NYC Big Book Award in Poetry Anthology, a Global E-Book Gold Award, the Elite Choice Gold Award, Book of Excellence Awards, the Queer Indie Lit Gold Award, and the 2021 International Reader's Favorite YA Paranormal Gold Award for quality and powerful storytelling. Her mission is to empower, enlighten, and entertain her readers with stimulating, inclusive, thought-provoking, character-based novels and transformative poetry that relate to modern-day issues and evoke an emotional response in her readers.

As an intuitive, alchemist, and energy activator, Lali intends to expand levels of consciousness by shining the light on sensitive subject matter to assist individuals in their healing journeys. She is an advocate for self-love, self-actualization, truth, freedom, equality, diversity, justice, unity, women, and children.

Award-Winning Publications by Lali A. Love

Heart of a Warrior Angel: From Darkness to Light (2019)
The De-Coding of Jo: Hall of Ignorance (2020)
The Joy of I.T: Infinite Transcendence (2020)
Ananda: Poetry for the Soul (2021)
The De-Coding of Jo: Blade of Truth (2021)

www.ingramcontent.com/pod-product-compliance
Lightning Source LLC
Chambersburg PA
CBHW020901080526
44589CB00011B/394